# My Paper Folding Book
# Easy Origami

**2**

# Basics of Paper Folding
Follow the instructions carefully before you start paper folding.

### Valley Fold
Take a square paper and fold it from the middle. Then, turn the folded paper as shown.

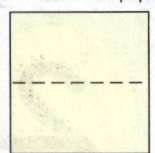

### Turn Over
Make a paper figure and turn it over as shown.

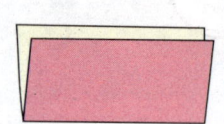

### Pocket Fold

① Fold the paper into the shape shown. Then fold into half from right to left.
② Now fold the top corner forwards and backwards to make a crease.
③ Then unfold as the crease is formed.

④ Fold the same top corner again.
⑤ Fold it to bring it down between the two layers as shown reversing its middle crease.
⑥ Your pocket fold is ready.

### Mountain Fold
Take a square paper and fold it in the middle. Now turn it in such a manner that the folded part is on the top as in the picture.

### Turn Upside Down
Make a paper figure and turn it upside down as shown.

### Fold in Front
Take a paper and fold it in the direction of the arrow.

### Making a Crease
Fold and unfold the paper in the required direction gently to get the desired fold. This is a crease.

### Squash Fold

① Make a mountain fold first. Fold into half and then unfold.
② Fold the top right corner forwards and backwards to make a crease and then unfold.

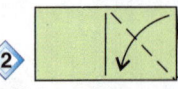

③ Press the top right corner from its upper edge.
④ Open out the corner into a flattened triangle.

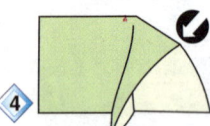

⑤ Your squash fold is ready.

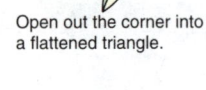

### Fold Backwards
Take a paper and fold it backwards as shown.

### Crease
A faint line which is the result of folding and then opening the fold.

Creased

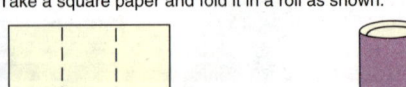

### Fold Over and Over
Take a square paper and fold it in a roll as shown.

### Stairstep Fold
As the name indicates, this fold is made by combining a Valley Fold and a Mountain to form a kind of pleat or stair step...

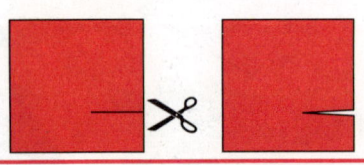

### Hood Fold

① Make the shape shown first and then fold into half from left to right.
② Fold the top corner forwards and backwards to make a crease.
③ When you fold the top, it will look like this.

④ Now fold the top corner at the crease inside out...
⑤ .... and reverse its middle.
⑥ Your hood fold is ready.

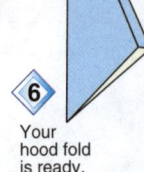

### Cut
Use a pair of scissors to make cuts neatly.

### Symmetrical Crease (1)
For a shapely crease, use your thumb-nail as shown in the diagram.

### Enlarge
Whenever a thick arrow is used as an indicator, it means that the next diagram is an enlarged one.

 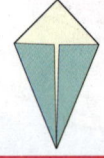

a swollen arrow

### Symmetrical Crease (2)
For a shapely crease, use your nail as shown in the diagram.

# Tall Hat

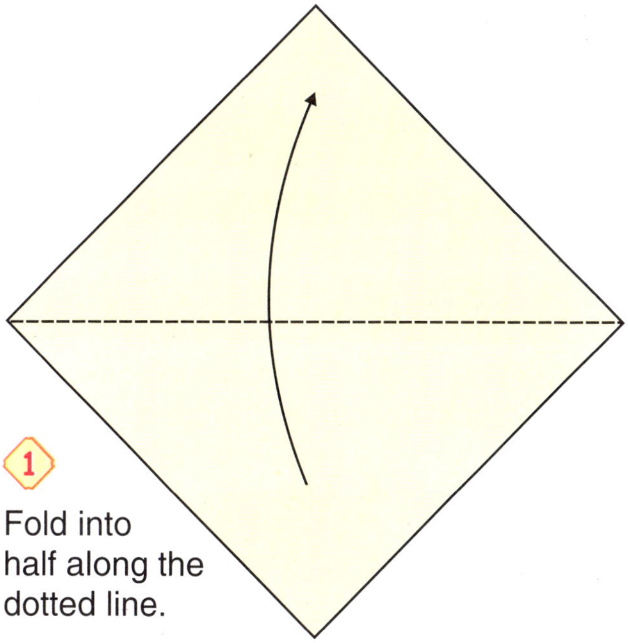

1. Fold into half along the dotted line.

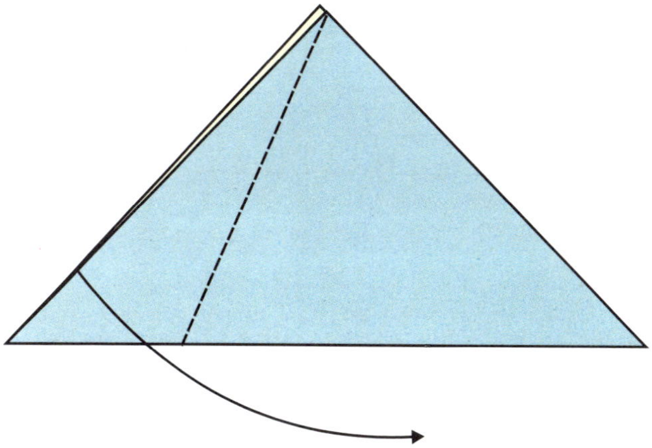

2. Fold along the dotted line in the direction of the arrow.

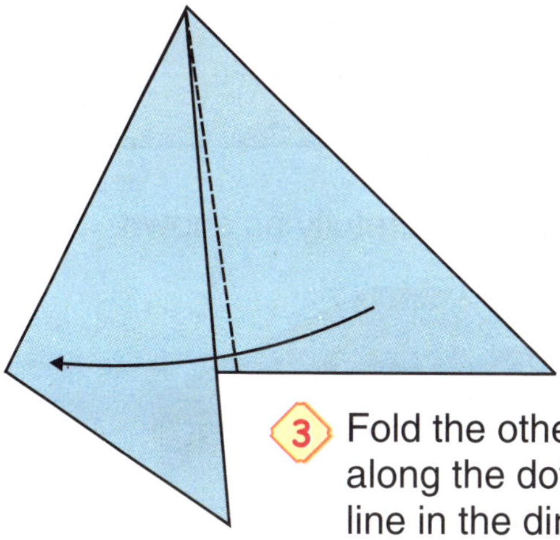

3. Fold the other side along the dotted line in the direction of the arrow.

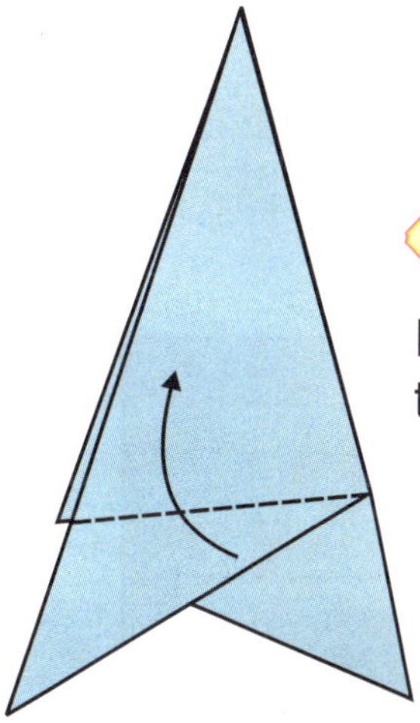

4. Fold the corners along the dotted line upwards.

5. Place your fingers inside and create a gap.

6. Your tall hat is ready to be worn.

# Slide

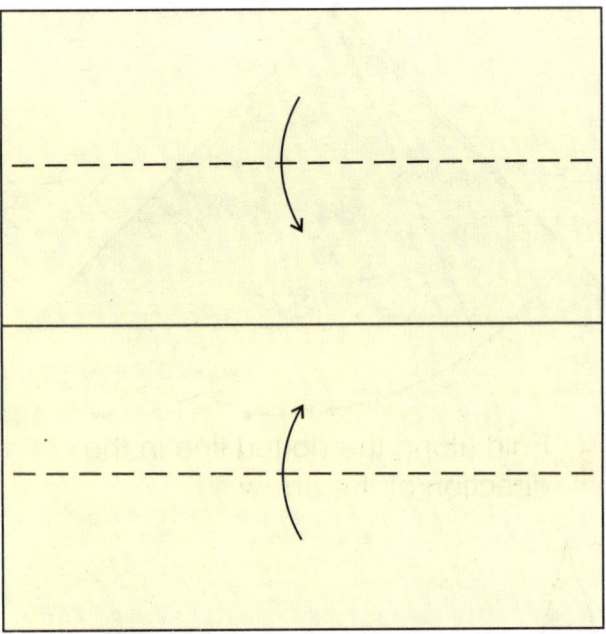

1. Fold the top and bottom edges to the centre line.

2. Your paper figure will look like this. Stick the joint with a tape.

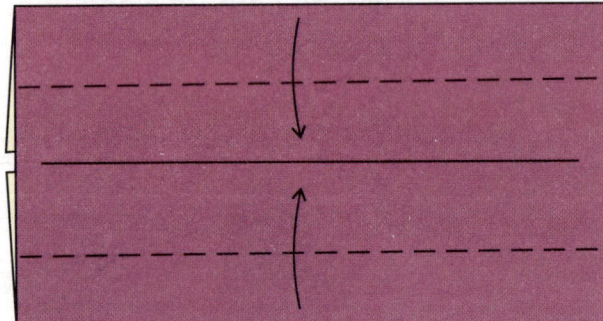

3. Turn your paper figure. Fold as shown in the step and crease firmly. And turn it over.

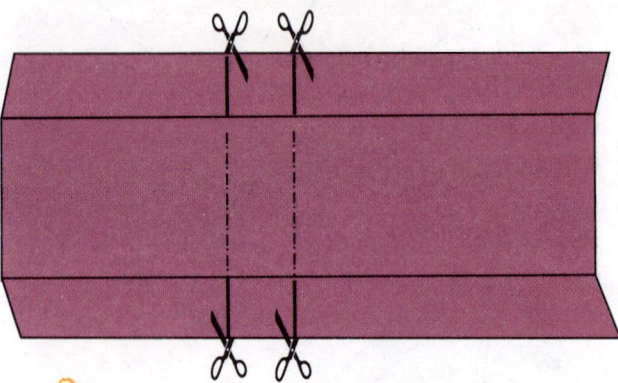

4. Make cuts carefully as shown.

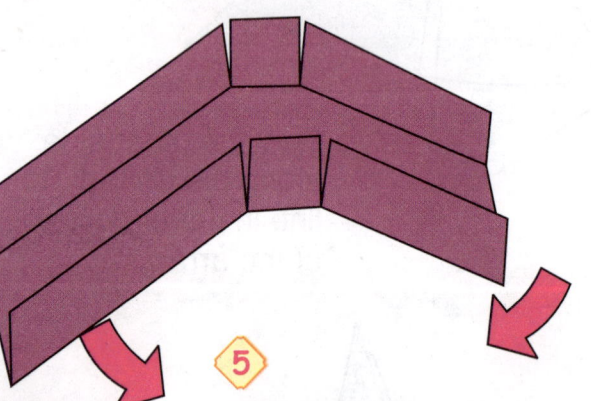

5. Fold the end portions backwards.

6. Make it stand on a hard surface and your slide is ready.

# Necktie

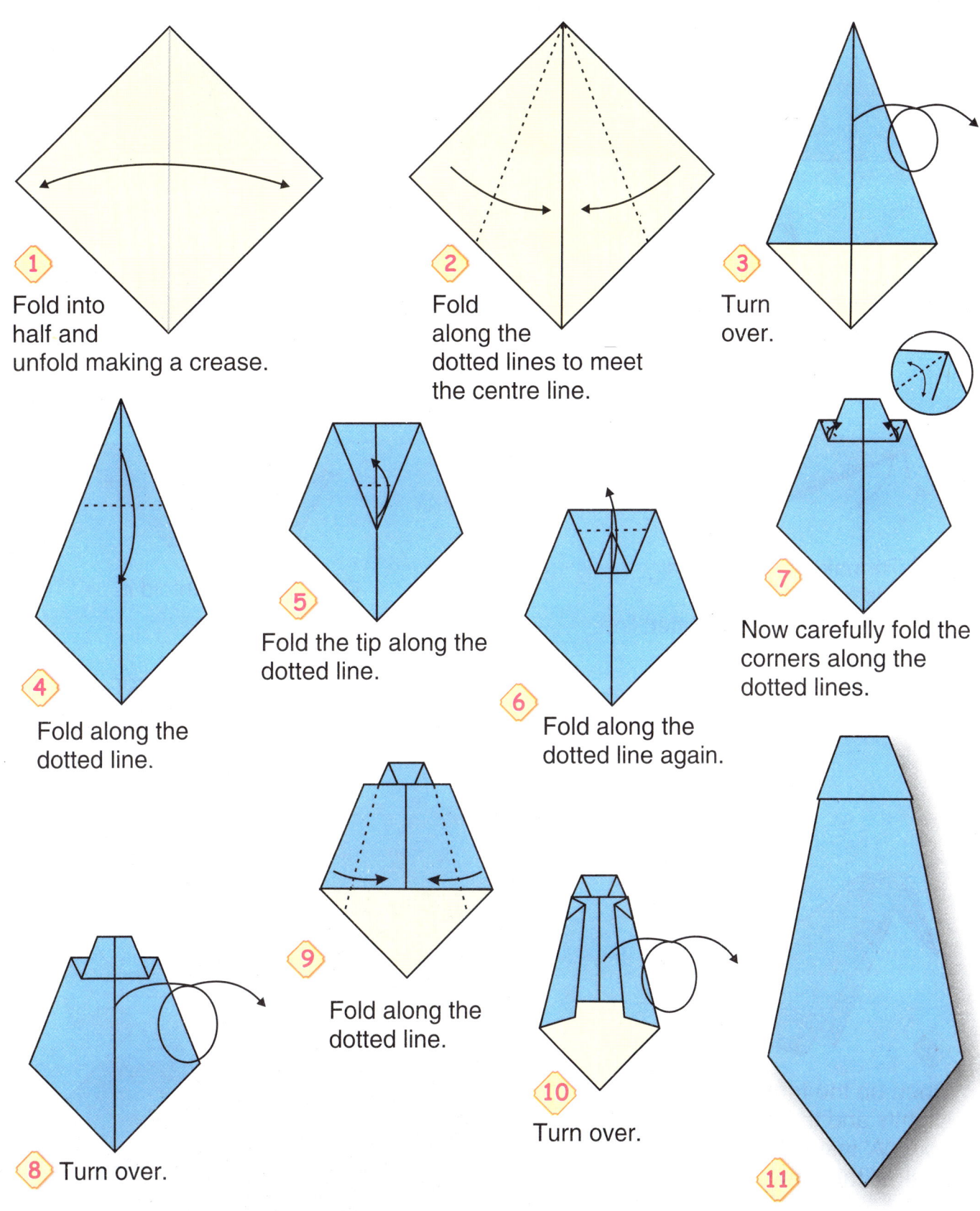

# Crow

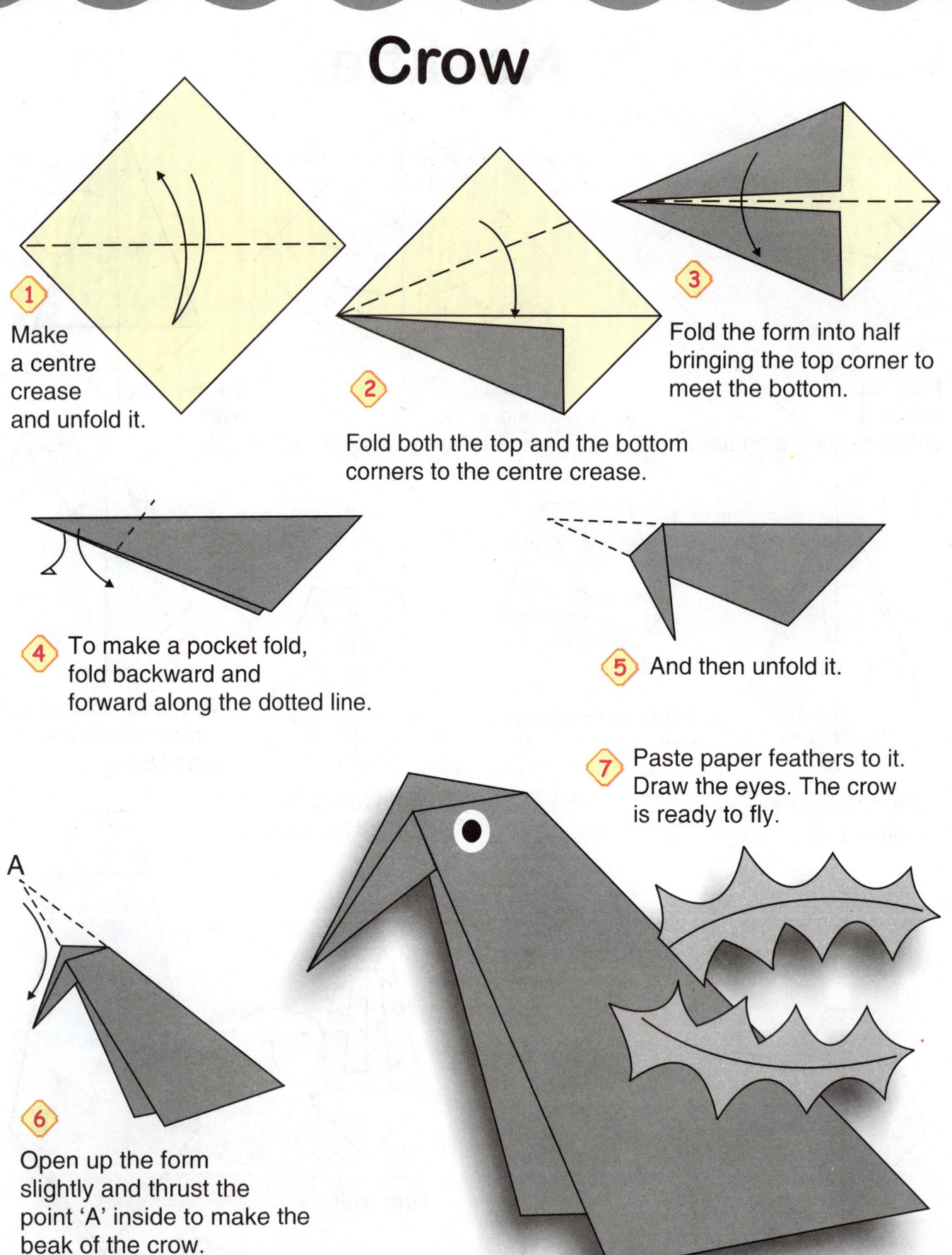

1. Make a centre crease and unfold it.
2. Fold both the top and the bottom corners to the centre crease.
3. Fold the form into half bringing the top corner to meet the bottom.
4. To make a pocket fold, fold backward and forward along the dotted line.
5. And then unfold it.
6. Open up the form slightly and thrust the point 'A' inside to make the beak of the crow.
7. Paste paper feathers to it. Draw the eyes. The crow is ready to fly.

# Swan

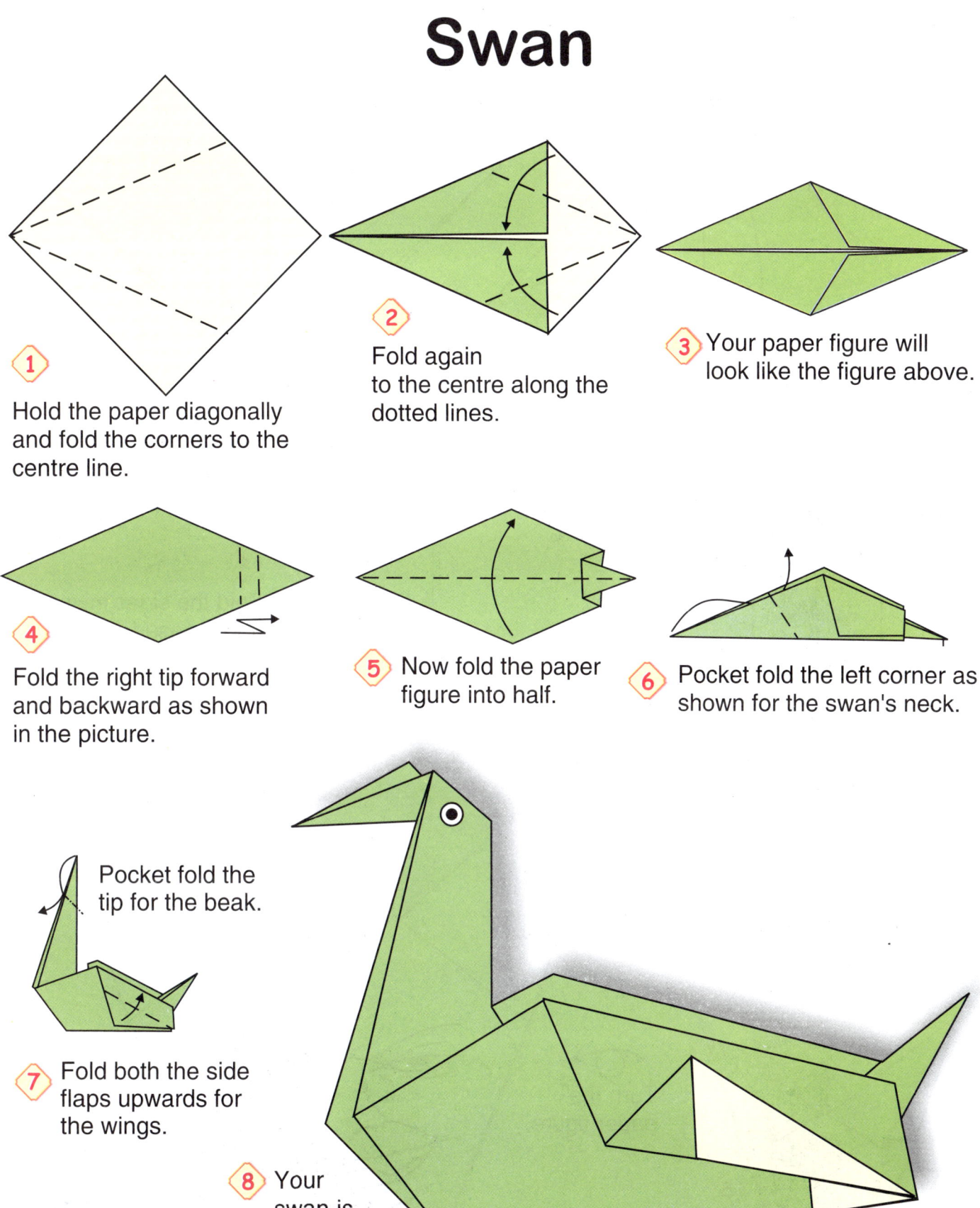

1. Hold the paper diagonally and fold the corners to the centre line.
2. Fold again to the centre along the dotted lines.
3. Your paper figure will look like the figure above.
4. Fold the right tip forward and backward as shown in the picture.
5. Now fold the paper figure into half.
6. Pocket fold the left corner as shown for the swan's neck.

Pocket fold the tip for the beak.

7. Fold both the side flaps upwards for the wings.
8. Your swan is ready to swim.

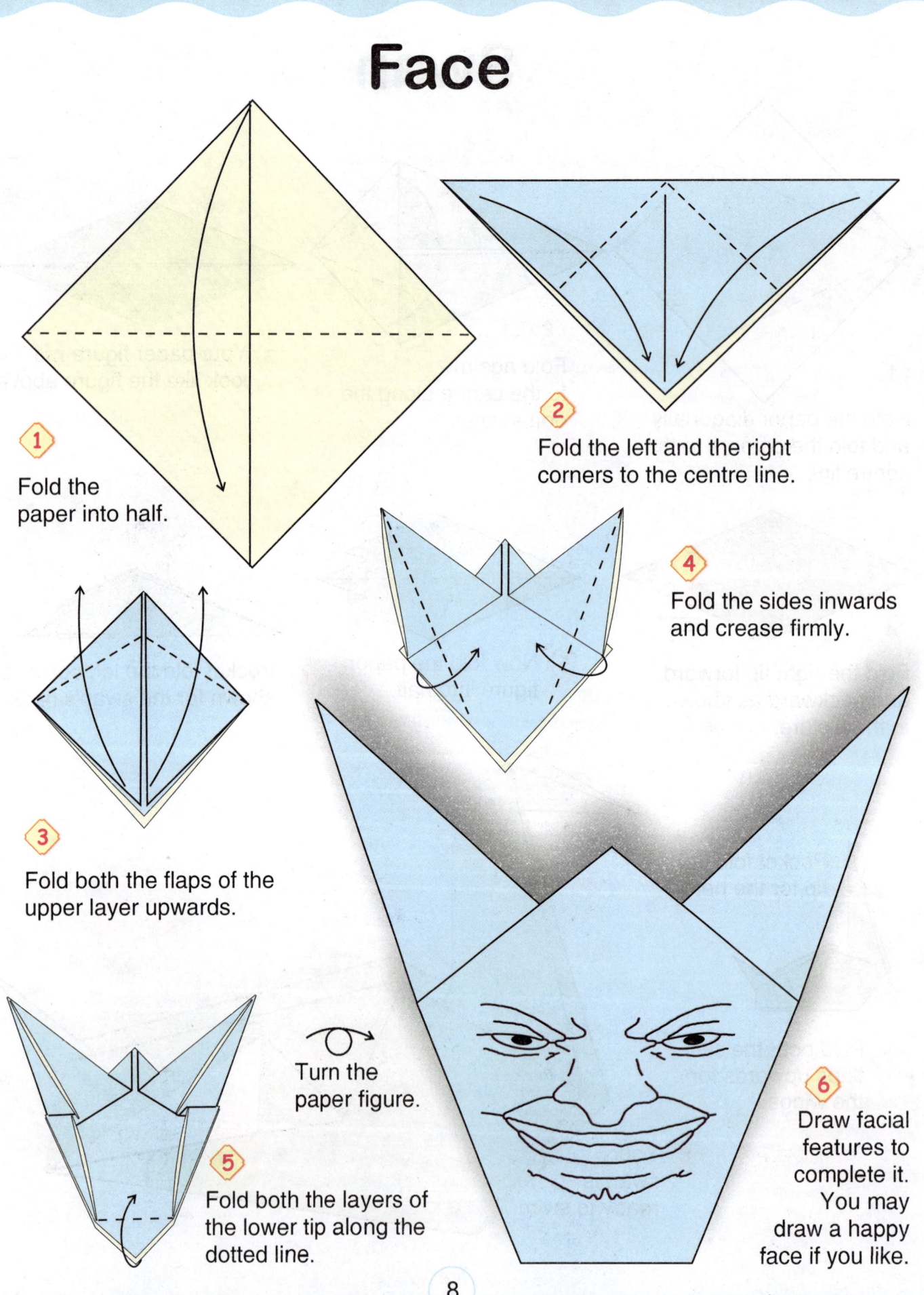

# Doll

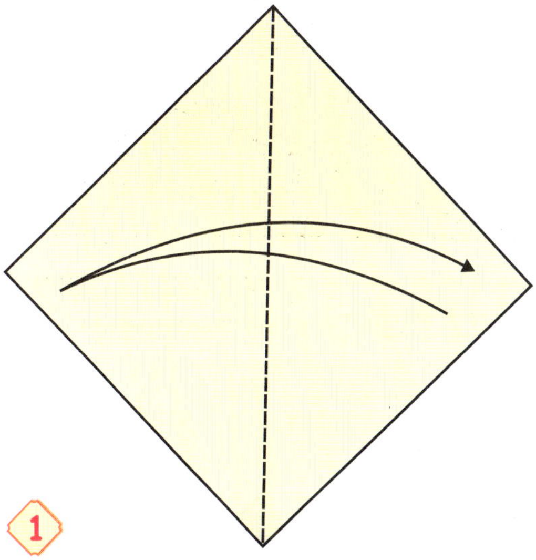

**1** Fold into half and unfold to make a centre crease.

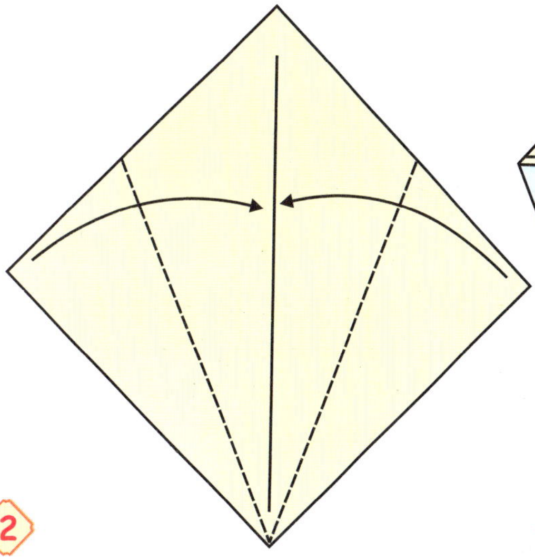

**2** Fold the left and the right corner to the centre crease.

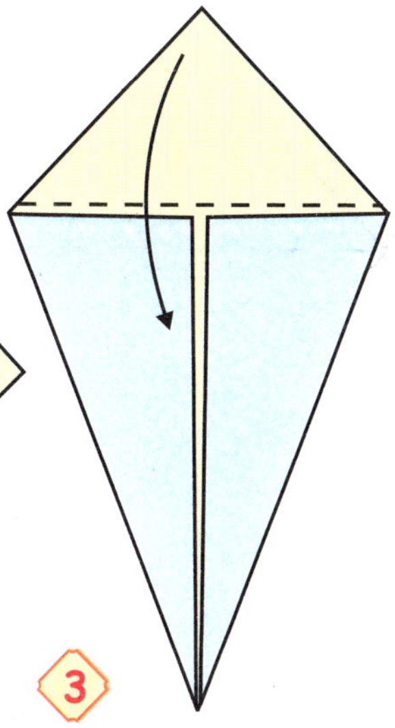

**3** Fold the upper flap downwards.

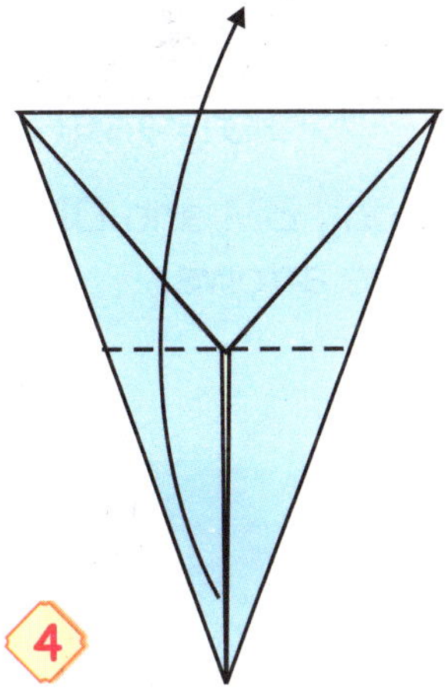

**4** Fold the lower corner upwards along the dotted line.

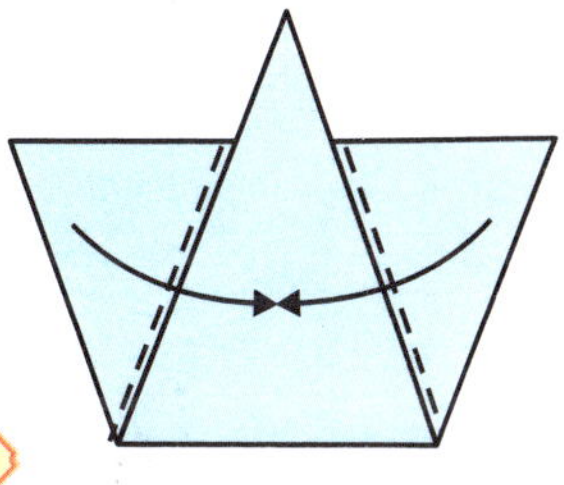

**5** Fold neatly the right and the left triangles to overlap each other.

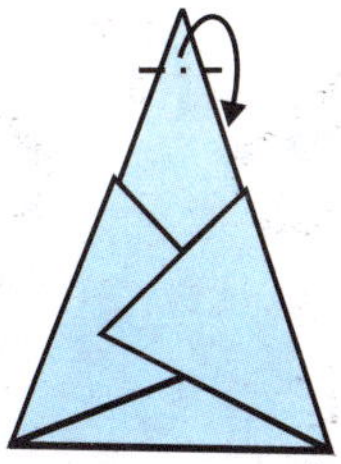

**6** Turn the tip backwards.

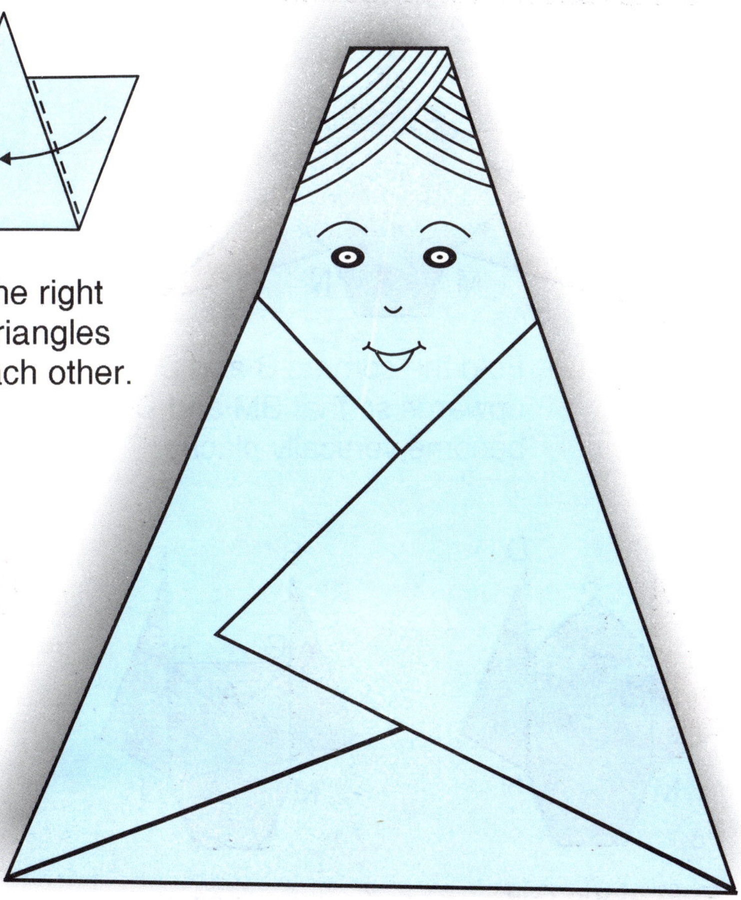

**7** Draw the eyes, hair and a smiling mouth to complete your doll.

# Wolf

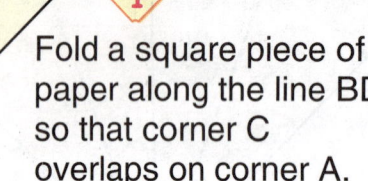

1. Fold a square piece of paper along the line BD so that corner C overlaps on corner A.

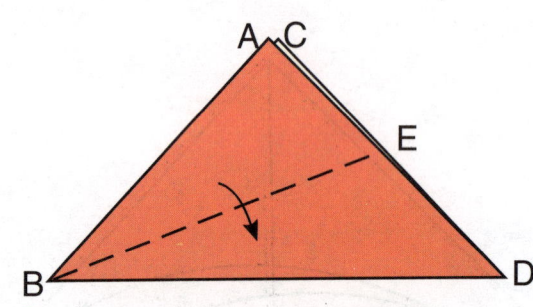

2. Create BE by folding BC and BA along the dotted line.

3. Cut two triangles at M and N as shown.

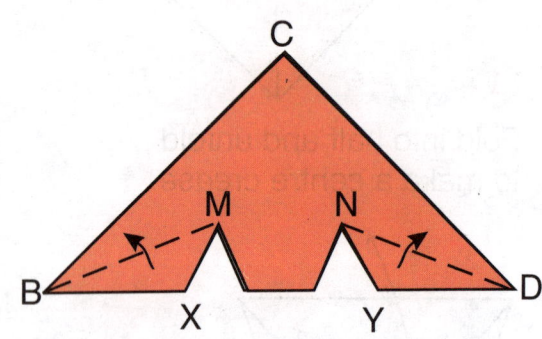

4. Fold along BM and DN along the arrows.

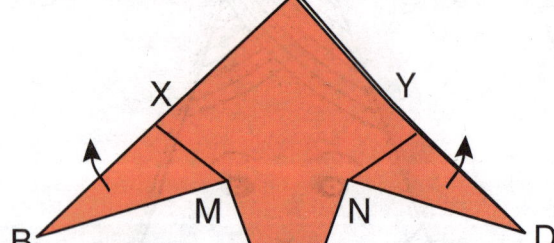

5. Fold the corners B and D upwards so that BM and DN become vertically placed.

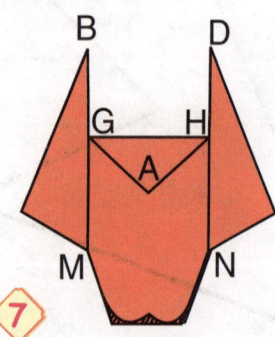

6. Fold along GH bringing corners C and A forward.

7. Turn the paper over and cut out the mouth as shown.

8. Draw the eyes, nose and cheeks of the wolf.

# Bat Mask

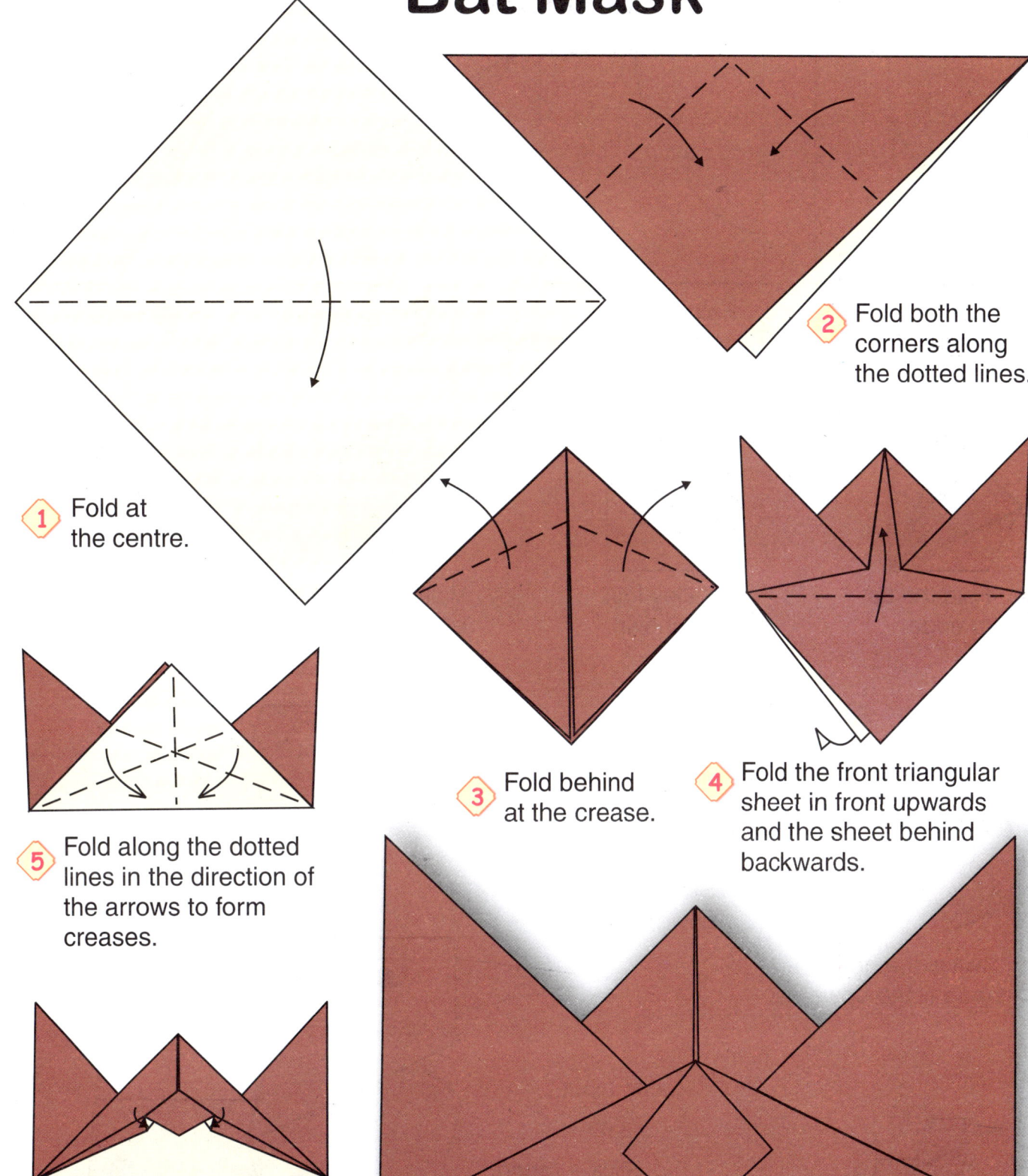

1. Fold at the centre.
2. Fold both the corners along the dotted lines.
3. Fold behind at the crease.
4. Fold the front triangular sheet in front upwards and the sheet behind backwards.
5. Fold along the dotted lines in the direction of the arrows to form creases.
6. Open the folds and make a diamond shape as shown in the above figure.
7. Your bat mask is ready to be worn.

# Duck

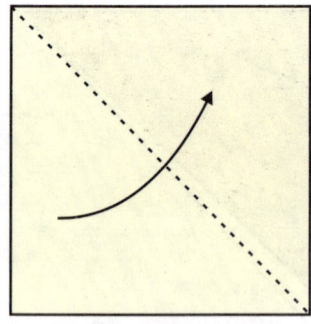 ① Fold into half diagonally.

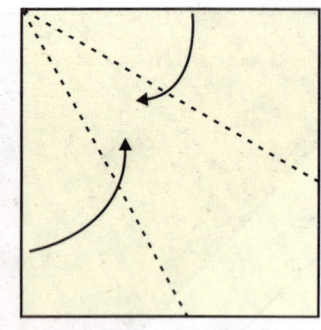 ② Fold both the corners to the centre.

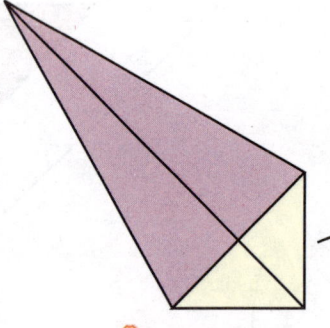 ③ Turn over.

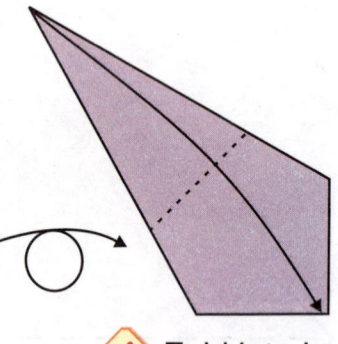 ④ Fold into half.

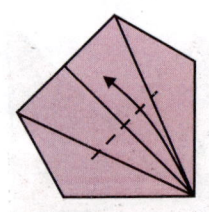 ⑤ Fold the tip to edge.

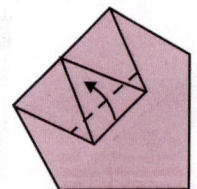 ⑥ Valley fold as shown.

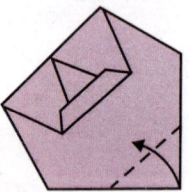 ⑦ Valley fold the tip in the direction of the arrow.

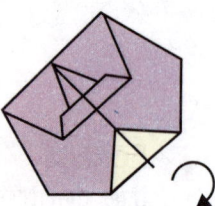 ⑧ Mountain fold into half.

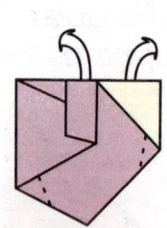 ⑨ Swivel the head and tail the upwards.

 ⑩ Swivel the bill downwards.

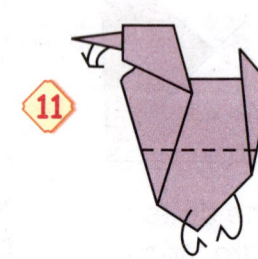 ⑪ Fold the bottom flaps inside.

 ⑫ Fold back the corner inside along the dotted lines.

 ⑬ Stick a round white paper for the eye and draw the eye ball.

# Heart

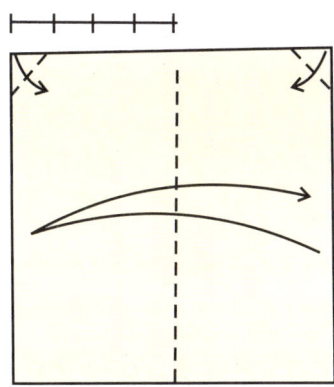

① Fold into half and unfold. Fold the top corners slightly.

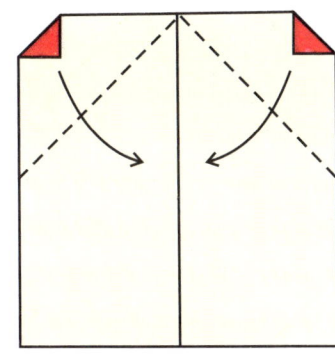

② Now fold them to the centre line.

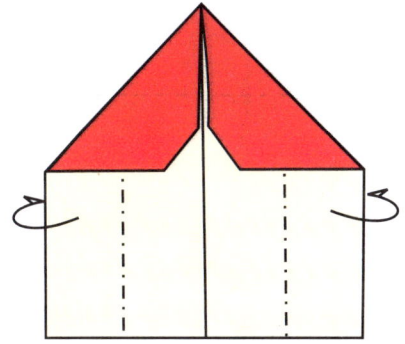

③ Fold the left and the right edges to the centre line backwards.

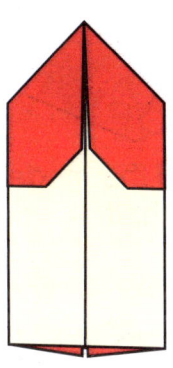

④ Turn it.

⑤ The paper figure should look like this.

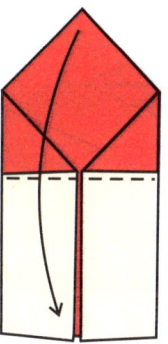

⑥ Now fold the paper figure into half.

⑦ Pocket fold the top corners

⑧ Fold the two corners (yellow) inside.

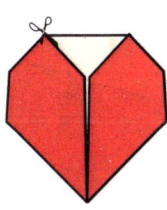

⑨ Cut the V shaped portion on the top.

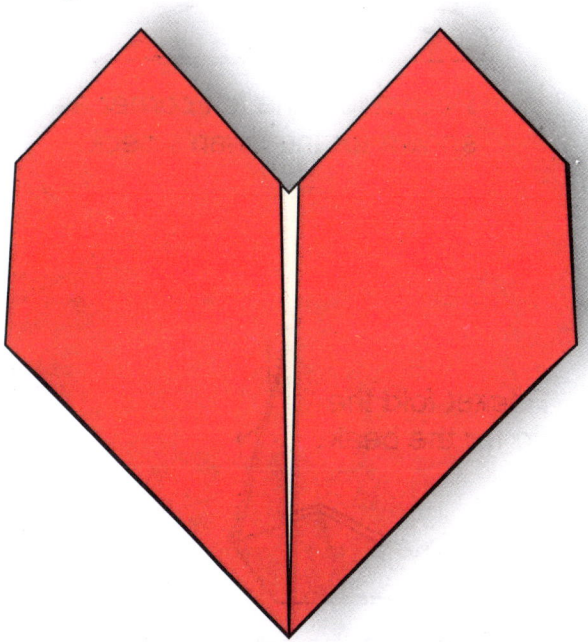

⑩ The heart is ready to beat.

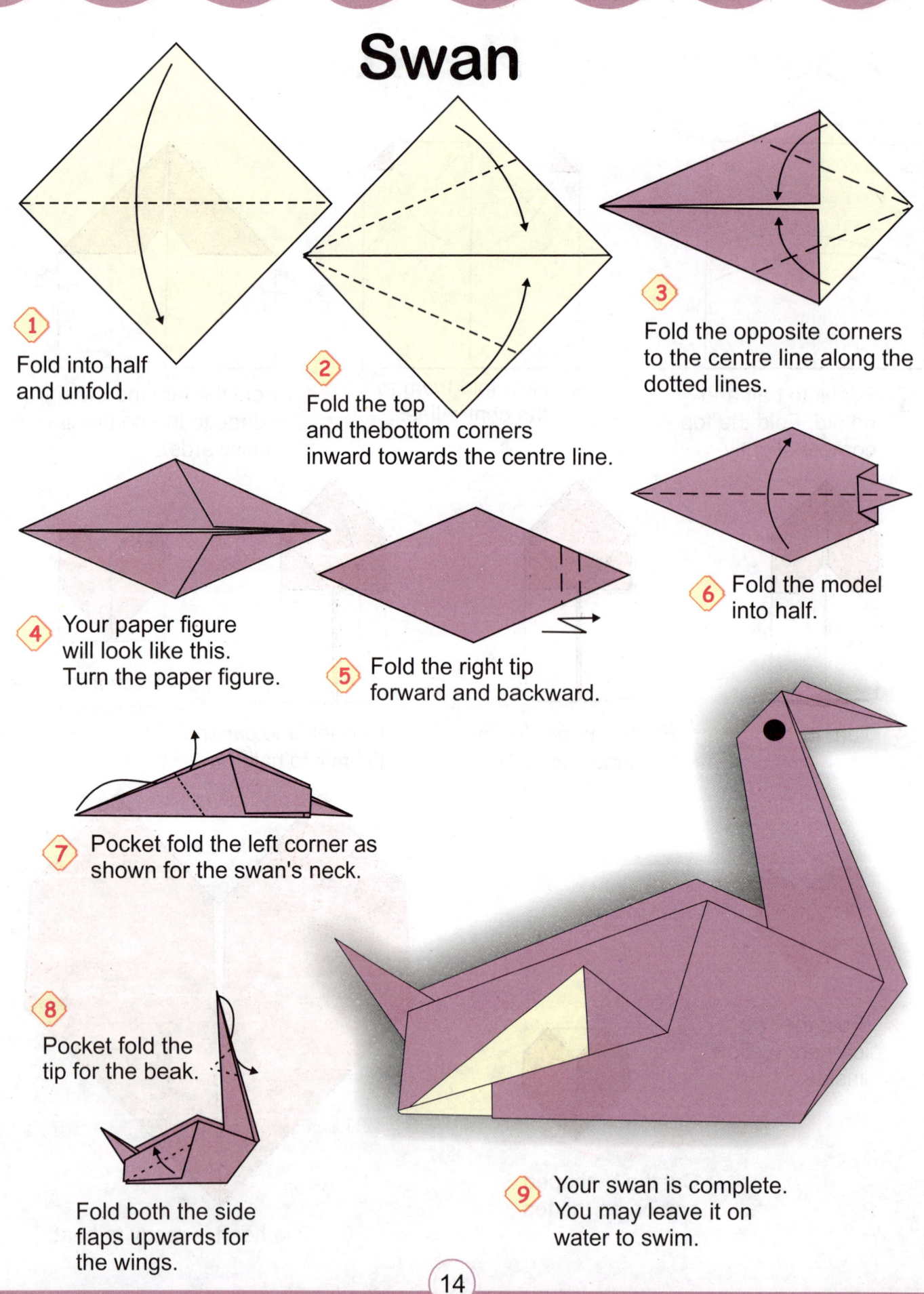

# Peacock

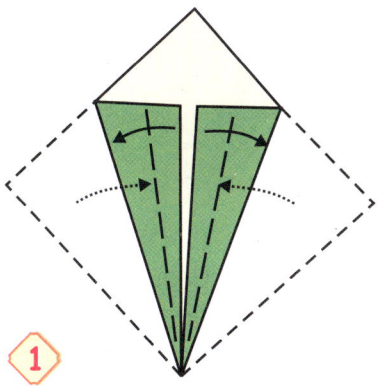

**1** Fold the opposite corners to form the shape shown.

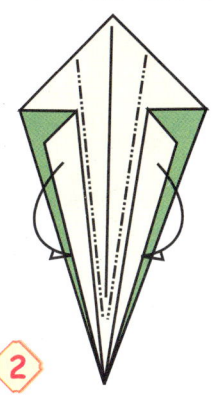

**2** Now fold the corners outwards.

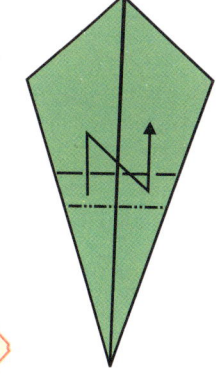

**3** Turn the paper figure. Fold behind to make a stair step fold.

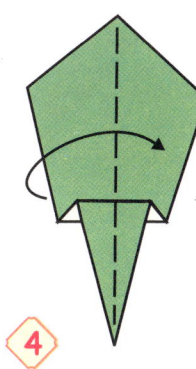

**4** Fold into half at the centre.

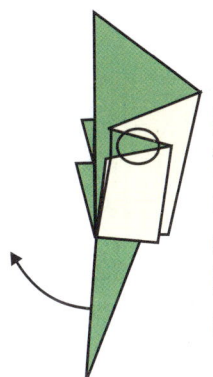

**5** Hold the paper firmly at the point marked with a circle and pull the bottom side ways as shown.

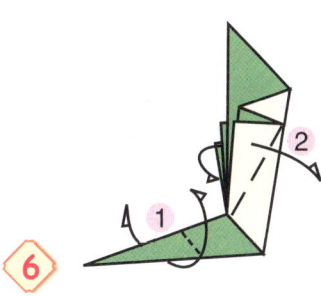

**6**
(1) Make a pocket fold for the beak.
(2) Pull out th triangle from the dotted line to form the peacock's feather.

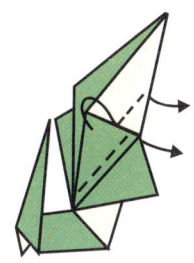

**7** Make a pocket fold on the rear side like the one on the front.

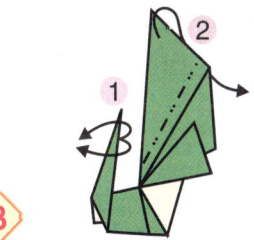

**8**
(1) Make a hood fold along the crease.
(2) Fold both the sides behind along the crease.

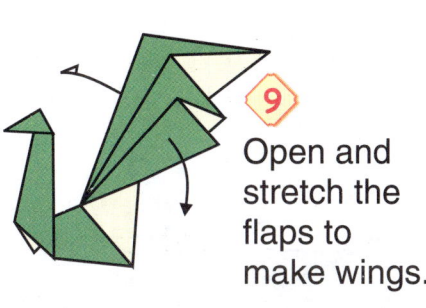

**9** Open and stretch the flaps to make wings.

**10** Your peacock is ready to dance in the rain.

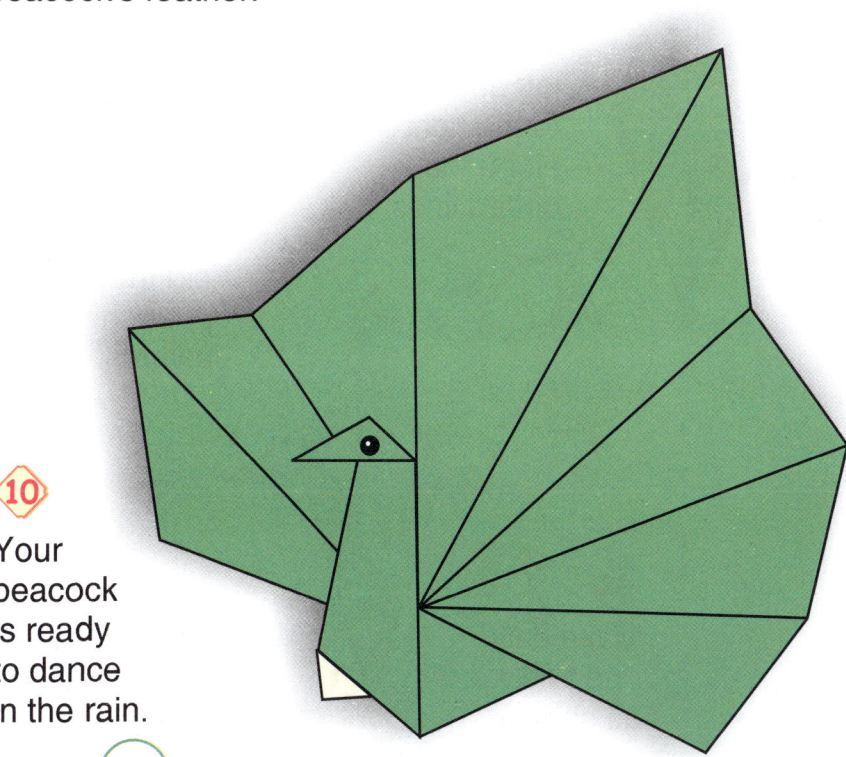

15

# Racoon

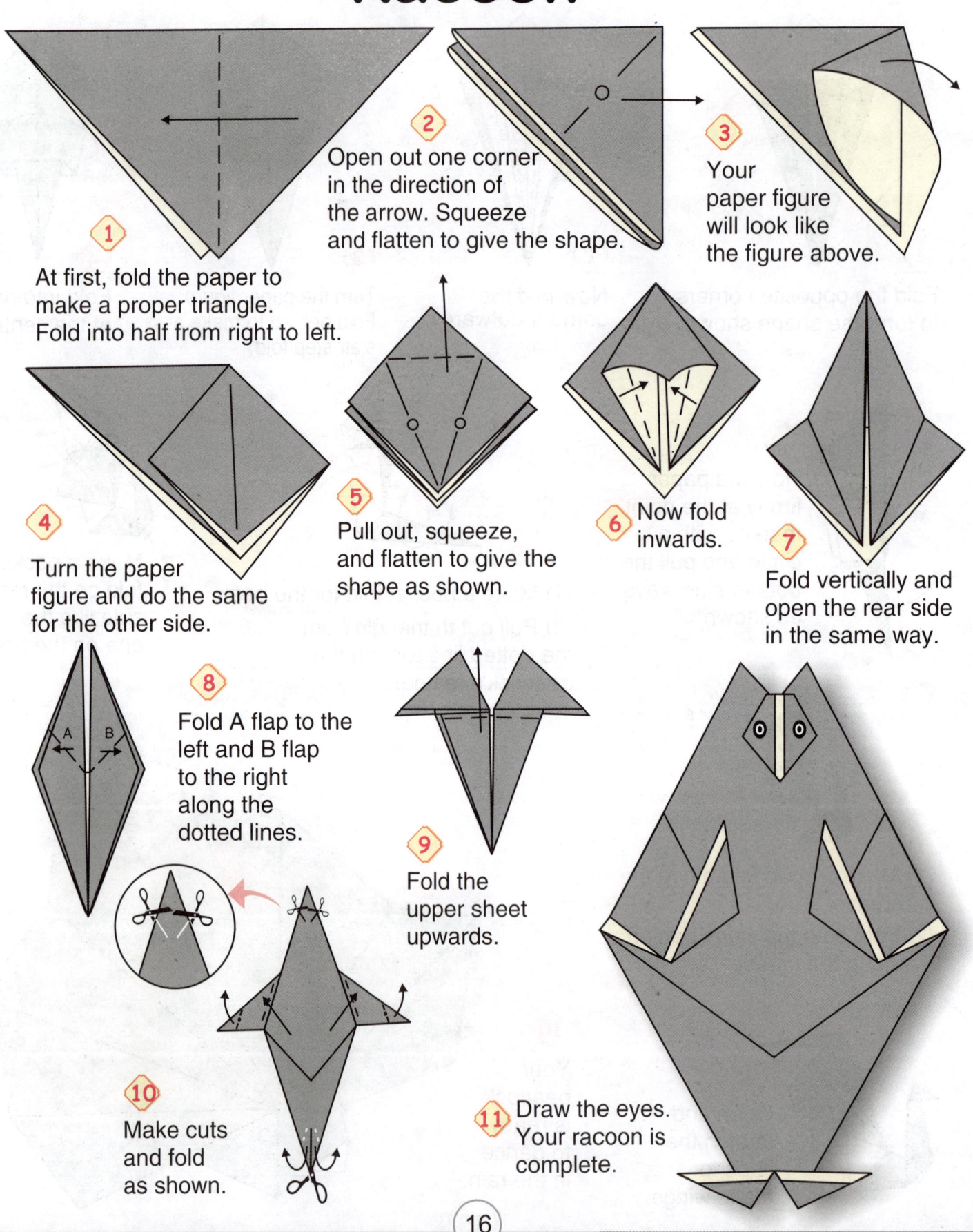

# Santa Claus

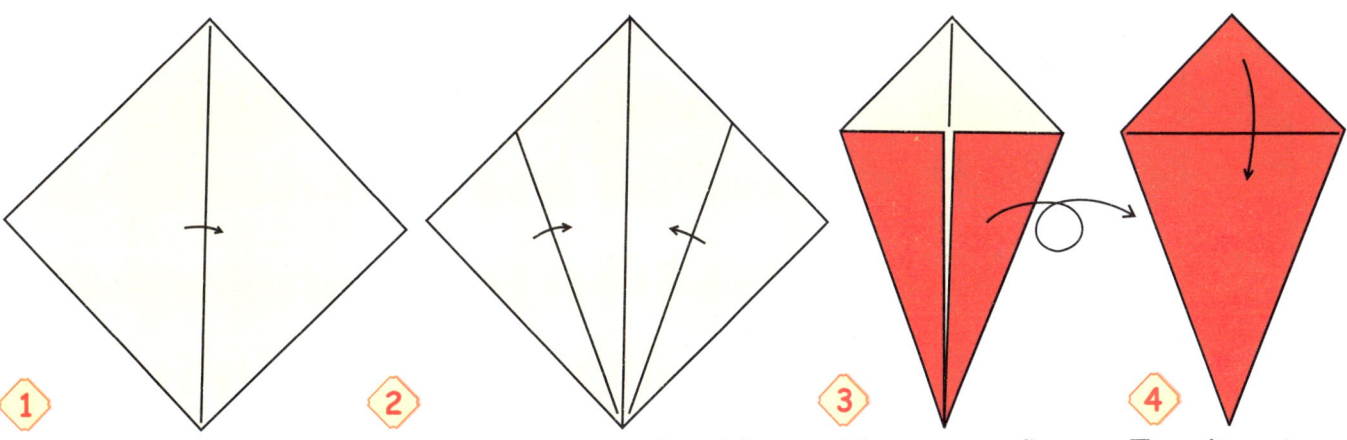

1. Spread the paper after making centre crease.
2. Fold the two opposite sides in the direction of the arrows.
3. Your paper figure will look like this.
4. Turn it over.

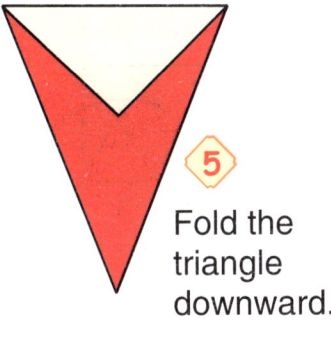 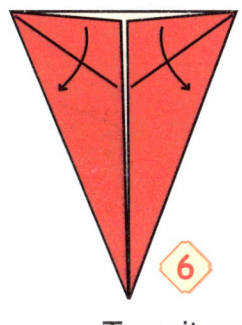 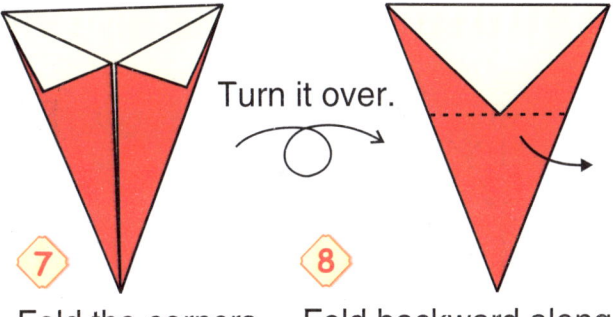

5. Fold the triangle downward.
6. Turn it over.
7. Fold the corners as shown.
8. Fold backward along the dotted line.

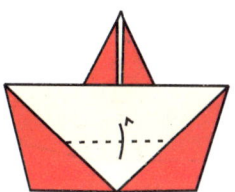 

9. Fold the triangle upward along the dotted line.
10. Again, fold the triangle outward along the dotted line.
11. Fold from A and B points along the dotted line.

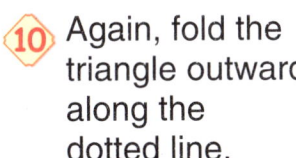   

12. Fold backwards from CD and EF in the direction of arrows.
13. Fold the paper backwards along the dotted line.
14. Draw eyes, nose and the mouth of the Santa Claus.
15. Attach a star at the tip of the cap and your Santa will be complete.

# Doll

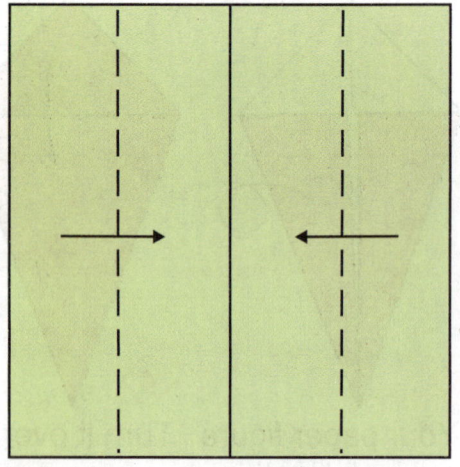

1. Fold both sides to the centre along the dotted lines.

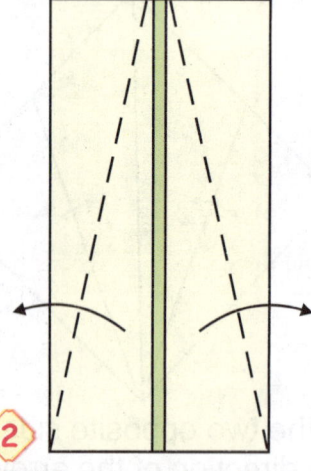

2. Fold outwards along the dotted lines.

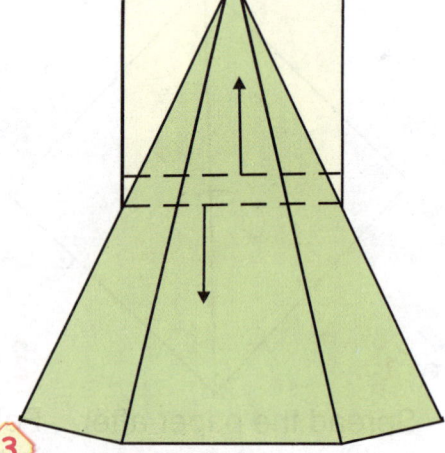

3. Now crease along the dotted lines for the shoulders.

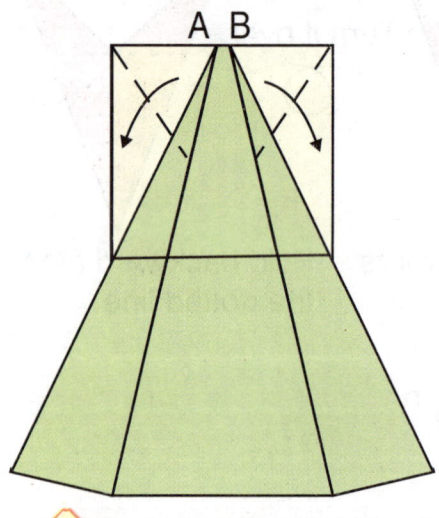

4. Fold from A and B points along the dotted lines in the direction of arrows.

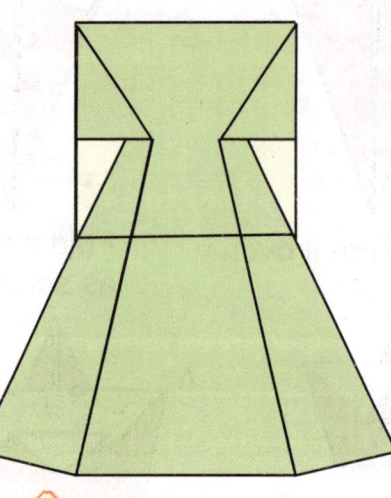

5. The paper figure will look like this.

6. Fold along the dotted lines in the direction of the arrows.

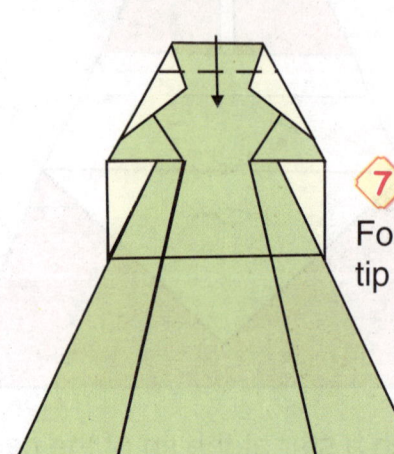

7. Fold the tip downwards.

8. Draw eyes, lips and nose to complete your doll.

# Elephant's Head

**1** Fold at the centre.

**2** Fold at the dotted line in the direction of the arrow.

**3** Fold along the dotted lines in the direction of arrow.

**4** Fold the corner inwards.

**5** Now fold the lower corner upwards in the direction of the arrow.

**6** Fold the top corner downwards.

**7** Make stairsteps to form the trunk of the elephant.

**8** Your elephant's head is complete!

# Love Bird

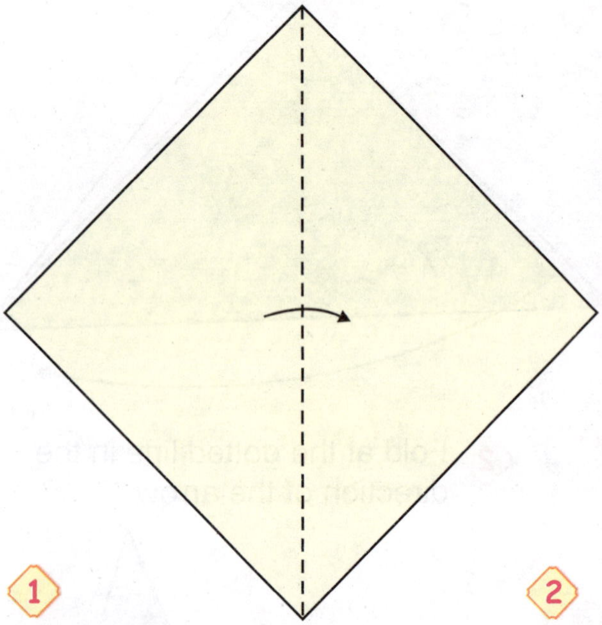

**1** Fold the paper into half along the dotted line.

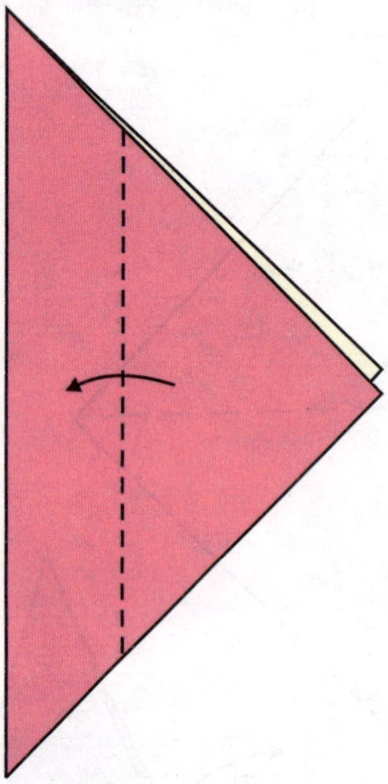

**2** Fold outwards along the dotted line in the direction of the arrow.

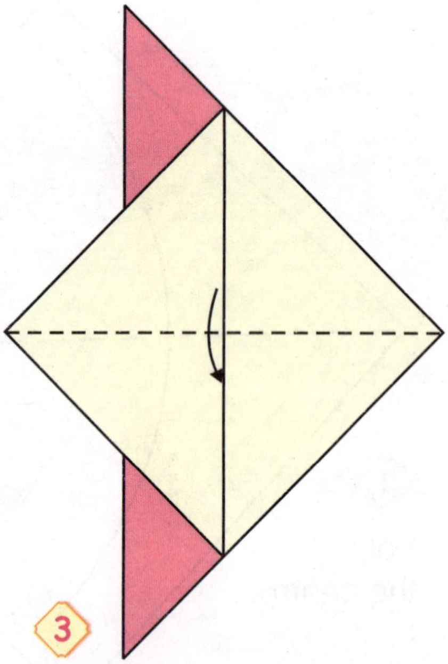

**3** Fold the figure into half to the centre along the dotted line.

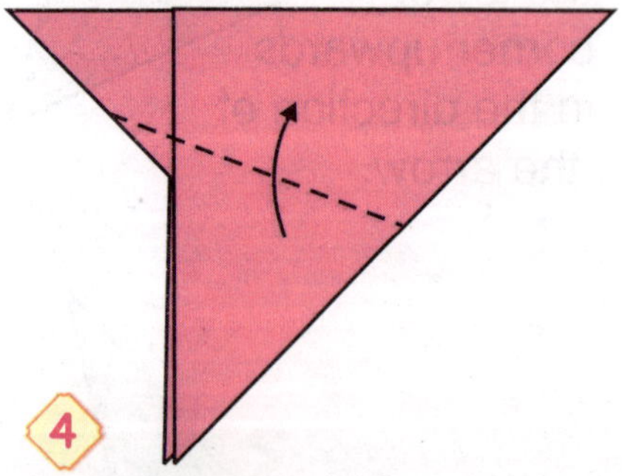

**4** Fold the flap upwards along the dotted line.

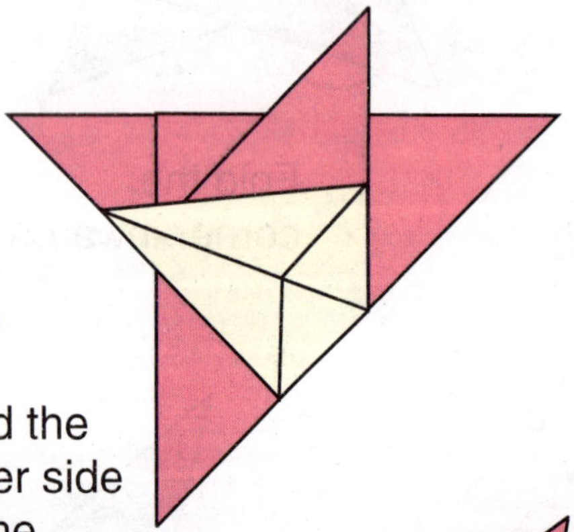

**5** Fold the other side in the same way.

**6** To make the beak fold the flap backwards along the dotted line.

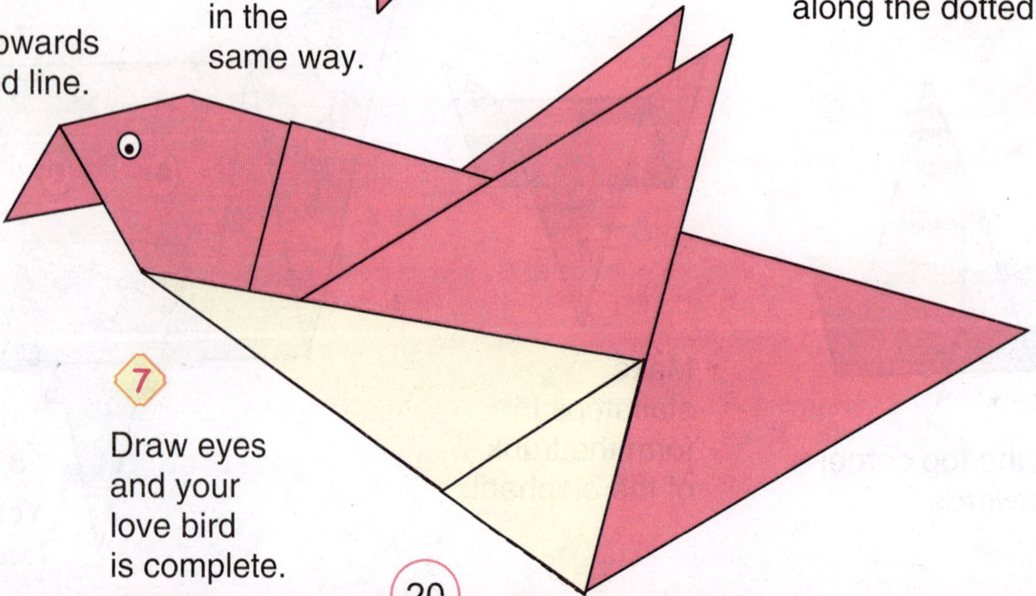

**7** Draw eyes and your love bird is complete.

20

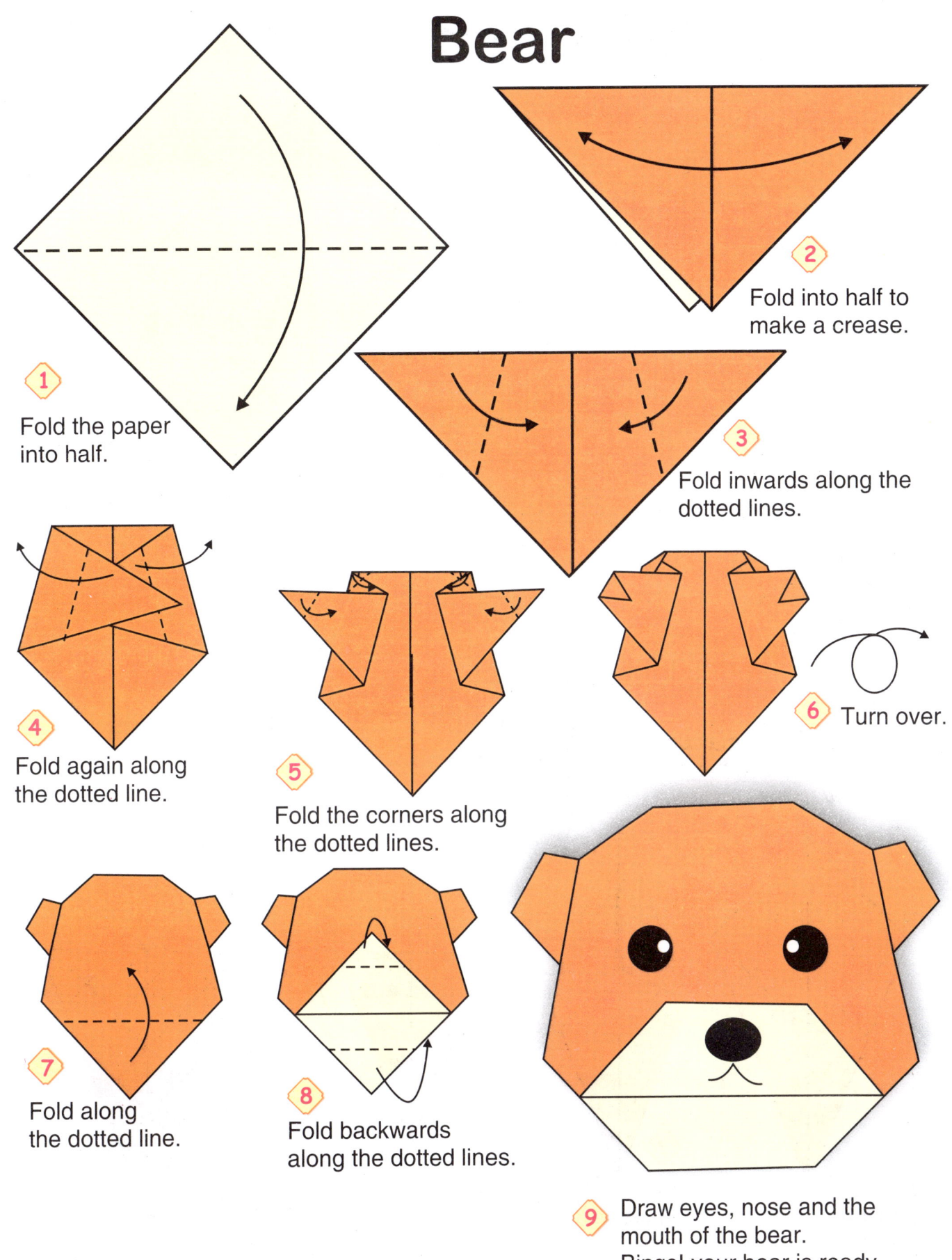

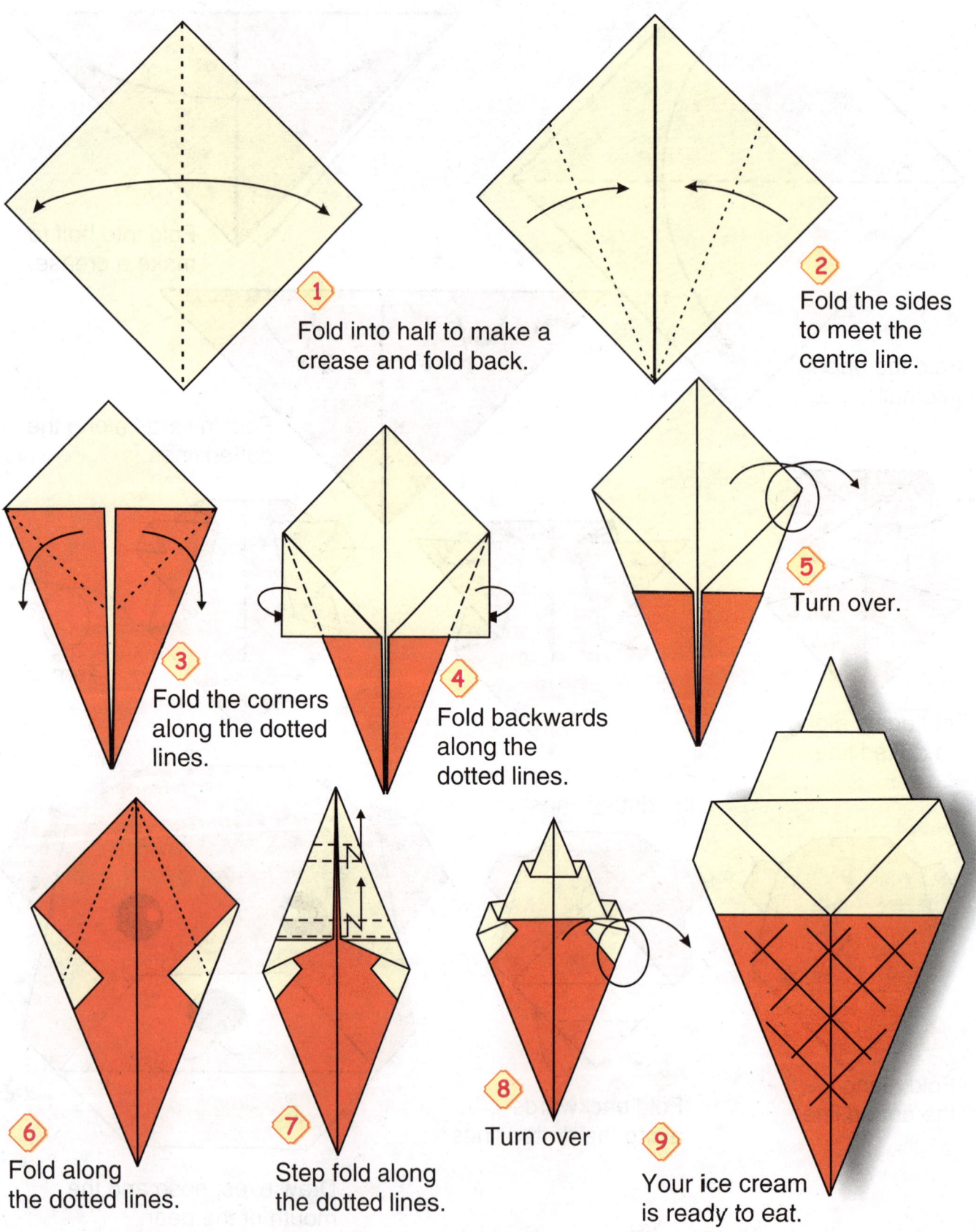

# Lady Bug

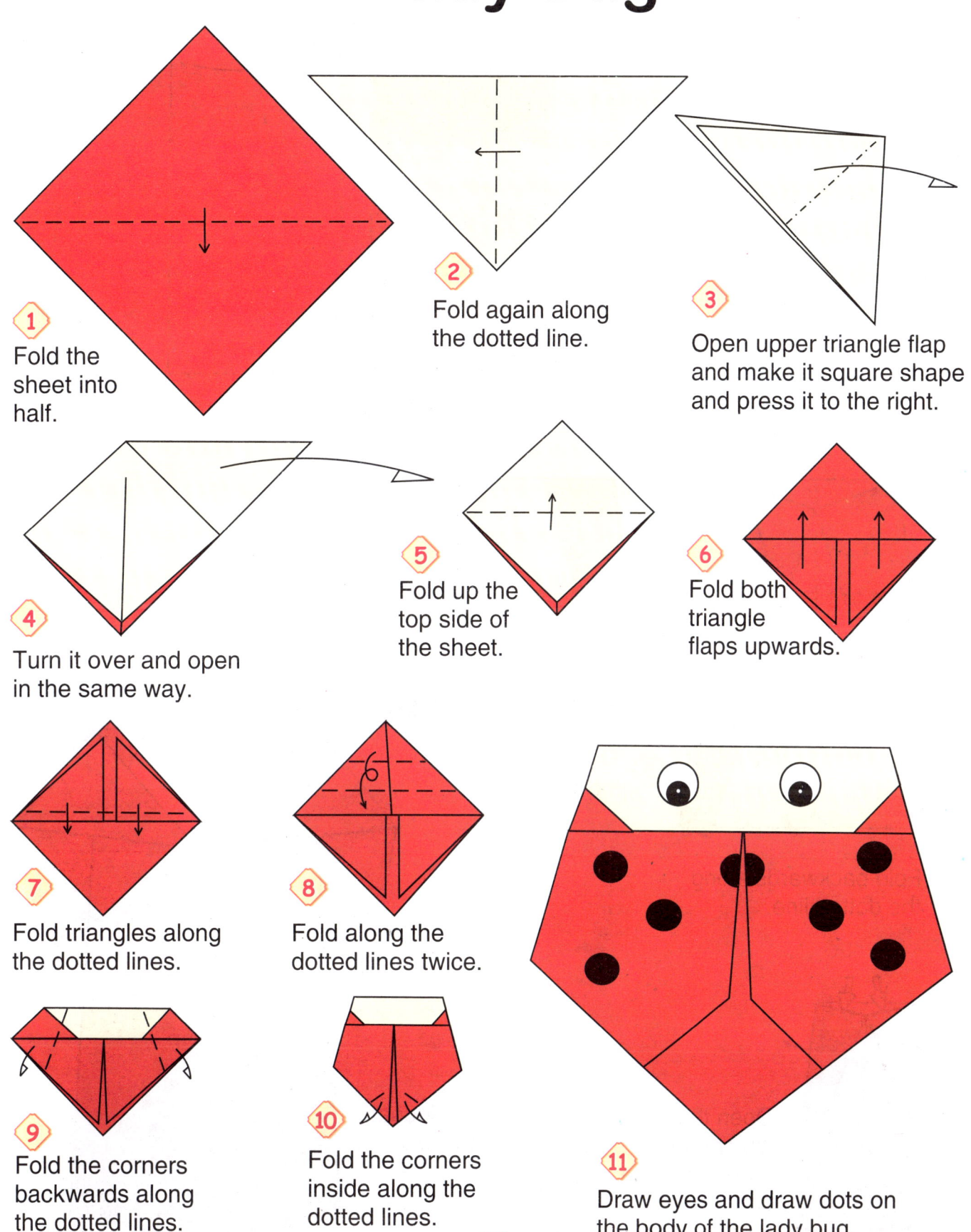

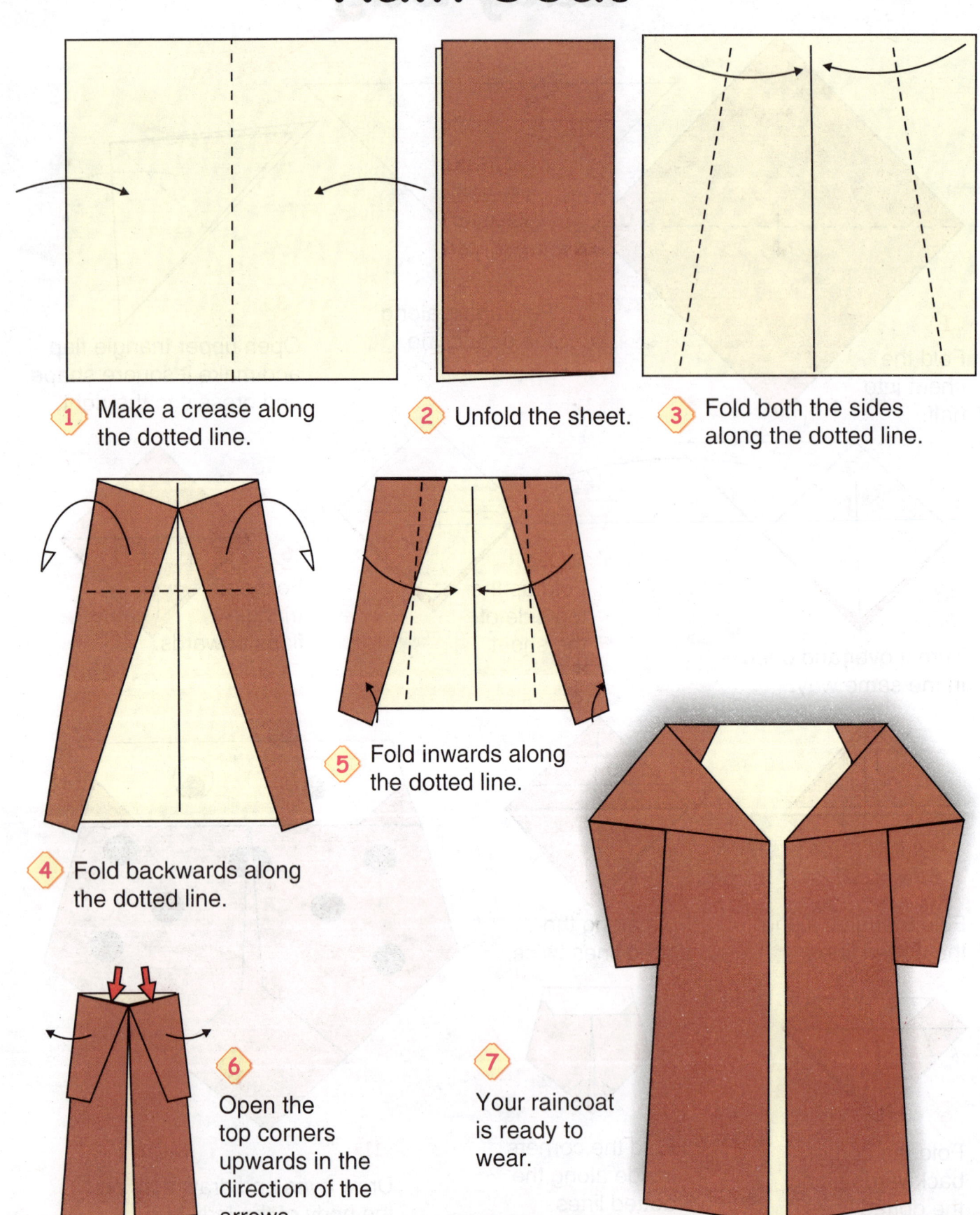